# *Shaping* TOMORROW

HOW TODAY's WORDS FRAME YOUR FUTURE

A 30-DAY DEVOTIONAL

27 26 25 03 02

*Shaping Tomorrow: How Today's Words Frame Your Future*

ISBN 13: 978-1-937578-82-4


Published by Capps Publishing
P.O. Box 10
Broken Arrow, OK 74013

cappsministries.com

# Shaping TOMORROW

HOW TODAY's WORDS FRAME YOUR FUTURE

A 30-DAY DEVOTIONAL

CHARLES CAPPS
WITH ANNETTE CAPPS

CAPPS PUBLISHING

# CONTENTS

# FOREWORD

As I reviewed this devotional, editing and writing the scripture declarations for each day, my own faith was strengthened, and I was reminded of the powerful principles that changed the entire course of the life of my dad, Charles Capps, and our entire family.

I also realized that if I do not keep these principles before me and remind myself of them continually, they seem to slip. When these teachings from the Word slip then I have a tendency to revert back to not applying them.

It is my hope that you will read and apply these principles from scripture that are revealed in both the New and the Old Testament. Indeed, throughout the Bible we can see the power of words, hope, and the creative power of calling things that are not as though they were.

This has not been a one-time read or study for me. It helped me so much to focus on these principles that I asked for a copy of my original first draft back (when it was taken to editing) because I missed feeding every morning on these writings, meditating on the scripture foundation, and speaking the words of faith that I wrote to accompany the daily meditation.

I am not sure if it is a "bad confession" or not, but I felt like I had become addicted to this manna of the Word, this bread from heaven that tells me who I am and the greatness of the One I serve.

Every believer is capable of building a strong faith that sustains them through the adverse circumstances of life. My dad's mission was to teach people to "put the Word of God to work in the everyday circumstances of their life." I assure you this strong faith is not out of reach, but easily obtainable as you apply the Word one day at a time. To apply it, you must speak it out loud.

May the God of our Lord Jesus Christ, the Father of glory grant you eyes to see and ears to hear and understand the marvelous inheritance you have received from Him.

Forever in Him,

Annette Capps

Day

1

# Do You Really Believe Everything You Say?

**MARK 11:23–24 KJV**

**23 For verily I say unto you, That whosoever shall say unto this mountain, Be thou removed, and be thou cast into the sea; and shall not doubt in his heart, but shall believe that those things which he saith shall come to pass; he shall have whatsoever he saith.**

**24 Therefore I say unto you, What things soever ye desire, when ye pray, believe that ye receive them, and ye shall have them.**

I was reading these verses one day, and I said, "Lord, I got that. I have preached it and preached it. I've got it all."

"No," He said, "You don't have it."

I kept reading it and reading it.

After a while, there was a phrase that just jumped off the page at me. It says, *"Those things which he saith."* I thought it was just talking about what you said to the mountain. You believe and doubt not in your heart. No, we must believe every word we speak releases faith.

When I started releasing faith in every word that I spoke, it was a different world out there. I quit telling jokes to exaggerate and put myself in a situation that I was not in. Some people thought I had gone just a little bit too far. I think my wife thought that for a while. It made a change in things when I started watching what I said.

You release faith in every word. Faith comes by hearing and hearing and hearing by the Word of God. We need to watch every word that we speak out of our mouth.

## God's Word for You Today

**PSALM 141:3**

**Set a guard, O Lord, over my mouth; keep watch over the door of my lips.**

## Give Voice to God's Word

*"I refuse to give the devil a foothold in my life. I speak only those words that are true to God's Word and in agreement with what He says about me."* (Ephesians 4:27, 29; Philippians 4:8)

Day

2

# Write the Word of God on Your Heart

Proverbs speaks about writing things on the table of your heart.

**PROVERBS 3:3**

**Let not mercy and truth forsake you; bind them around your neck, write them on the tablet of your heart,**

You cannot write the Word of God on your heart with pen and ink. How are you going to do it?

The psalmist tapped into it when he said:

**PSALM 45:1**

**...my tongue is the pen of a ready writer.**

You can write your words on the table of your heart by speaking them out of your mouth. You write the Word of God on your heart with your tongue.

There is power in the words you speak. God's words are full of power, and He has faith in His Word.

I get amused at some of the faith critics when they say things like, "Those faith people tried to make the Word into God."

Well, why in the world would we want to try to do that when God has already said, *"In the beginning was the Word, and the Word was with God, and the Word was God"* (John 1:1).

God's Word is still over every situation in life, whether you believe it or whether you don't believe it. But if you do not apply the Word, it won't be over every situation in your life. God's Word has to be abundant in your heart and applied to your words. Jesus said:

**MATTHEW 12:35**

**A good man out of the good treasure of his heart brings forth good things, and an evil man out of the evil treasure brings forth evil things.**

He is not talking about the blood pump but about the core, the center of your being. The good man brings forth good things out of his heart. Evil comes the same way. It comes out of the heart.

What you put in your heart is going to get into your mouth. The more you say it, the more you believe in it. What you speak with your mouth is going to get into your heart and eventually manifest in your life.

## God's Word for You Today

**ROMANS 10:17 ESV**

**So faith comes from hearing, and hearing through the word of Christ.**

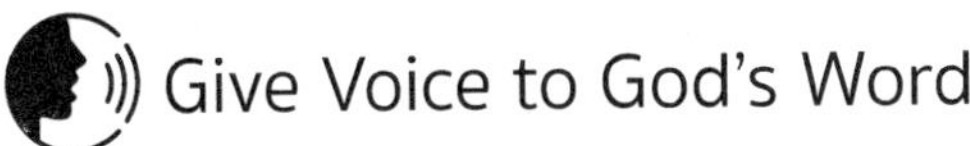

## Give Voice to God's Word

*"The peace of God that passes all understanding keeps my heart and mind through Christ Jesus. And things which are good, and pure, and perfect, and lovely, and of good report, I think on these things."* (Philippians 4:7–8)

Day

3

# Words Are Like Seeds You Plant in the Ground

There is nothing more revealing than the parable of the sower. Jesus said:

**MARK 4:14**

**The sower sows the word.**

It is obvious that the Word of God is the seed because Jesus went on to say:

**MARK 4:26**

**...The kingdom of God is as if a man should scatter seed on the ground,**

You are the one who plants the seed, which is the Word. This is how the kingdom of God works. You speak the Word of God and plant it in your heart.

I farmed for 29 years before I went into the ministry. I recognize the fact that the soil does not have dominion over the seed. When you plant a seed in the soil, that seed demands of that soil, and that soil has no choice but to respond to that seed.

I have a farm in England, Arkansas. It is a good Christian farm. But if somebody slipped in on it one night and sowed some marijuana on the backside of the field, do you think that the ground is going to say, "No, we are not raising marijuana. We are a good Christian farm?" No, it has no choice.

Jesus likened the heart of man to soil that will produce anything you plant in it. The words you speak are the seeds you are planting in your heart. If you're speaking in line with the Word and the promises of God, you are planting good seed.

One time, there was a minister driving me to the motel from the airport. I guess he had had a split in his church. He said, "Well, Brother Capps, every time you get the church going and the ministry going real good, the devil tears it up. He just throws a monkey wrench in the deal and just splits the church. Every time, doesn't he?" and he started nodding his head.

I said, "No, in my ministry, he doesn't because no weapon formed against me will prosper! Whatever I do will prosper!"

He said, "Oh, my God."

He did not realize what he was doing. He said, "It happens every time." He believed for it. That was his confession. Nothing else can happen in his ministry but that. It is going to happen periodically as long as he talks that way. He is planting the seed.

Don't blame someone else if you plant dandelions in your yard and they come up. Just quit planting them. Poison them and cancel them out. Words are seeds that are spoken, and if you have spoken wrong words, just delete them!

## God's Word for You Today

**EPHESIANS 4:29–30 ESV**

**29 Let no corrupting talk come out of your mouths, but only such as is good for building up, as fits the occasion, that it may give grace to those who hear.**

**29 And do not grieve the Holy Spirit of God, by whom you were sealed for the day of redemption.**

## Give Voice to God's Word

*"I let no corrupt communication come out of my mouth, but that which is good to edifying that it may minister grace to the hearer. I grieve not the Holy Spirit of God, who has sealed me unto the day of redemption."* (Ephesians 4:29–30)

Day

4

# God's Promises Belong to You

**HEBREWS 11:1**

**Now faith is the substance of things hoped for, the evidence of things not seen.**

If you have evidence in a court of law, it has to exist. Faith is the evidence of things hoped for. What is it we hope for? We have hope in the Word of God and His promises. Faith, then, is the evidence or the substance of that hope.

**2 CORINTHIANS 1:20**

**For all the promises of God in Him are Yes, and in Him Amen, to the glory of God through us.**

What does that mean? It means you can have faith in the promises of God. He has already said "yes" to every promise in the Book. God's promises belong to you! When Jesus died, He set this new covenant in motion by His blood. You don't get it when *you* die. You got it when *He* died.

Suppose your rich uncle owns 40 acres in downtown Dallas and makes you the sole heir. It would be kind of unusual if you come running home and tell your wife, "My uncle made me the sole heir of all of his estate in downtown Dallas. I can't wait to die to get it."

She will want to feel your fevered brow. No, you don't have to die to inherit your uncle's estate. He has to die. Then, you, as heir, receive it.

You do not have to die to inherit the promises of God. Jesus already died so you could receive the promises of God. God's promises are seeds, and you sow them with your words until they get down into your heart.

**ROMANS 10:8 NASB**

**But what does it say? "The Word is near you, in your mouth and in your heart" — that is, the word of faith, which we are preaching,**

The words, or the confession of your mouth, go together with belief in your heart.

## God's Word for You Today

**ROMANS 10:9–10 NASB**

**9 That if you confess with your mouth Jesus as Lord, and believe in your heart that God raised Him from the dead, you will be saved;**

**10 for with the heart a person believes, resulting in righteousness, and with the mouth he confesses, resulting in salvation.**

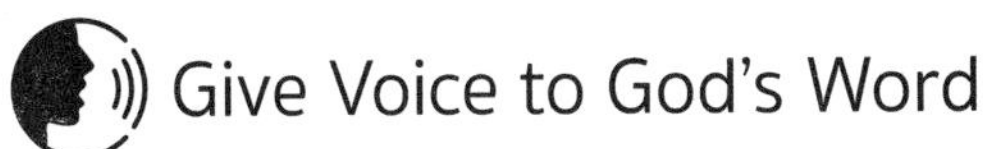

## Give Voice to God's Word

*"It is true unto me according to the Word of God."* (Psalm 119:25; Luke 1:38)

Day

5

# Your Faith Will Never Rise Higher Than Your Confession of the Word

Jesus taught us the law of faith when He said:

**MARK 11:23 KJV**

**For verily I say unto you, That whosoever shall say unto this mountain, Be thou removed, and be thou cast into the sea; and shall not doubt in his heart, but shall believe that those things which he saith shall come to pass; he shall have whatsoever he saith.**

I have been flying for 61 years, and the Lord gave me an illustration of how the law of faith works, like the physical laws that cause airplanes to fly. My airplane, when it is sitting on the runway and filled with books and luggage, weighs nearly four tons. I am expecting the natural physical law of lift to make that thing fly like a bird.

My airplane will not fly until I do something to put the law of lift into operation. I can sit there on the runway and look out on the wing, but no lift is there while I am sitting still. The law of lift is what causes that airplane to fly. I can pray for lift until the tires rot off the plane, but until I put the throttles to it and thrust it through the air, there will be no lift on the wing.

Your faith will never rise any higher than your confession of the Word of God. Until you push the throttles forward on that airplane, there is no lift. You can pray for faith until you faint from exhaustion, but faith will not come until you hear the Word and hear yourself speaking the Word because faith comes by hearing the Word of God.

Speaking God's Word will cause your faith to rise up and increase. When the airplane goes down that runway, the wings are designed to create their own lift. Your confession of God's Word creates faith the same way.

Going down the runway on a good hot day with a load, it takes all but about 200 feet of that runway to get my plane fast enough to fly. Why didn't I shut it off halfway down the runway and declare, "Flying doesn't work today?" I didn't shut it off because I have too much knowledge. The manufacturer's handbook tells me how many feet down the runway I will have to go at a certain temperature to create enough lift to fly like a bird. And it will do it every time!

There is a law of lift that causes my plane to fly. There is also a law of faith that is put into operation by the words you speak. Paul said:

**ROMANS 10:8 NASB**

**But what does it say? "The word is near you, in your mouth and in your heart" — that is, the word of faith which we are preaching,**

Verse 17 says, *"So then faith comes by hearing, and hearing by the word of God."*

If you superimpose those verses over each other, it is talking about you speaking the Word and hearing your voice audibly say what God said. It does something for your human spirit and to the core of your being that nothing else will do. It will change your life forever.

The biggest change in my life, other than being born again and filled with the Spirit, was when I began to voice the Word of God. I could tell you true stories of how many amazing things happened after I started planting good seeds instead of weed seeds.

## God's Word for You Today

**2 PETER 1:3**

**As His divine power has given to us all things that pertain to life and godliness, through the knowledge of Him who called us by glory and virtue,**

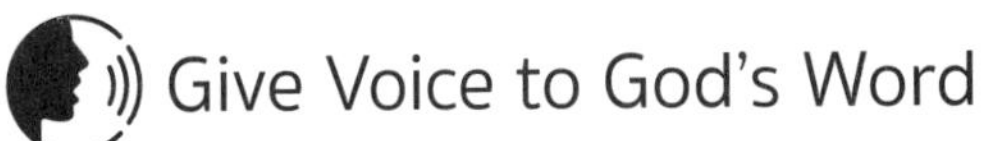

## Give Voice to God's Word

*"God is on my side. God is in me now, who can be against me? He has given to me all things that pertain to life and godliness. Therefore, I am a partaker of His divine nature."* (2 Corinthians 6:16; John 10:10; 2 Peter 1:3–4; Romans 8:31)

Day

6

# How Do You Measure Faith?

## God Gives Everyone the Measure of Faith

**ROMANS 12:3 KJV**

**...according as God hath dealt to every man the measure of faith.**

Somebody said, "Well, if He has dealt to everyone the measure of faith, why don't I have any?" It is because the measure of *your* faith is equal to the measure of the Word inside you.

Faith comes by hearing and hearing and hearing the Word. Paul said:

**ROMANS 10:8**

**But what does it say? "The word is near you, in your mouth and in your heart..."**

It did not say the Word was in your pastor's mouth and in your heart. It says it is in ***your*** mouth and heart.

When I went to school, we quoted the multiplication tables until we knew them by what? By heart. They knew back then that what you said audibly would get into your heart.

When you say something over and over again, it gets down in your heart. You don't have to think about two times two equals four. You just know it because it is in your heart.

Now, here is one of the missing links in the faith connection. How do you have a measure of faith? Do you have an ounce, or do you have a ton? The only way you can measure faith is by how much of God's Word abides in you. The Bible is the measure of faith that God has dealt to every man. And you get it into your heart by confessing it. God does not just give you faith.

When you plant a seed in the ground, before the sun can rise and set, the seed has demanded that your need be met. It takes time, but it will produce. You plant a seed, and you reap a harvest. This is the way Jesus always taught. He would take natural things and show you how spiritual things work. You sow a seed, and you reap a harvest.

Likewise, when you confess the Word, faith comes.

In the 1970s when the Word of God concerning faith and confession began to be taught, there were a lot of people who got the idea that all you have to do is say it, and it would happen like magic. They were disappointed because what they said did not instantly appear.

There is a lot more to faith than just saying it, but saying it is involved in working it. You have to say and say and speak and proclaim the Word until it gets inside you.

Jesus said it this way:

**JOHN 15:7**

**If you abide in Me, and My words abide in you, you will ask what you desire, and it shall be done for you.**

If the Word is abiding in you, you will speak the Word. Jesus also said, "Out of the abundance of the heart the mouth speaks." So when you are faced with problems in life, what comes out of your mouth? If the Word is in you, then faith-filled words will come forth, and you will speak to the problem, and it will obey you.

## God's Word for You Today

**Luke 17:6 NASB95**

**...If you had faith like a mustard seed, you *would* say... and it *would obey* you.**

## Give Voice to God's Word

*"The word of faith is in my heart and in my mouth. I speak to the problem of _______ in my life, and I say, 'Be plucked up from the roots and be planted in the sea! You obey me, in Jesus' name!'"* (Luke 17:6)

Day

7

# Calling for What You Don't Have — Healing

**1 PETER 2:24**

**Who Himself bore our sins in His own body on the tree, that we, having died to sins, might live for righteousness — by whose stripes you were healed.**

The Bible says, *"By whose stripes you were healed."* It uses the words "were healed." The word "were" means it is already done. If it says, "we were healed," it must mean ***we are healed*** as far as God is concerned. Right?

Why am I confessing "I am healed" when I am sick? When you say you are healed, you are calling for what you don't have.

God taught Abraham to call things that were not as though they were. He called himself the "father of many nations" when he did not have the promised child – before it came to pass.

People say, "Why, I just don't understand that. You are just lying if you say you are healed when you are sick."

No. You are not lying. You are calling for what you don't have!

You can do a little experiment along this line. The next time you are staying in a hotel, get on the elevator on the *first floor*, punch the button for the *first floor* and see what happens.

I have done it. I don't know how many times. I would get on the elevator on the fourth floor, punch the fourth-floor button, and wonder what was wrong with the elevator when it didn't move. But, it was not the elevator that had the problem. I punched the button for the fourth floor, and the elevator did not go anywhere because I was already on the fourth floor.

You can stay there and confess you are sick all day long and not get any better. You are calling it the way it is. As long as you say it like it is, the law of faith says it will stay the same.

The law of faith is the law of change. If you're going to say the same thing that exists, confessing the same thing, nothing is going to change other than it may get worse.

I found out that when you begin to speak the promise of God, it changes situations and circumstances.

## God's Word for You Today

**MATTHEW 8:17 NASB**

**This happened so that what was spoken through Isaiah the prophet would be fulfilled: 'He Himself took our illnesses and carried away our diseases.'**

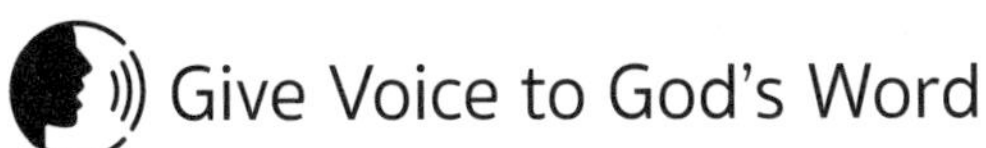

## Give Voice to God's Word

*"Jesus Himself took* **my** *illness and carried away* **my** *disease and pain. Therefore, I* **am** *well. I* **am** *whole. I* **am** *healed! I call my body healthy!"* (Isaiah 53:5)

Day

8

# The Shield of Faith

**EPHESIANS 6:16**

**...above all, taking the shield of faith with which you will be able to quench all the fiery darts of the wicked one.**

When you apply the Word of God by speaking it, there is a force field around you. When Peter walked down the street, there was a force field around him that was so strong the sick got healed as he walked by. It was not just the shadow of the sun; it was a force field of faith that surrounded him (Acts 5:15).

The Lord said to me one time, "You can build your shield of faith as strong as you want by confessing the Word."

He said, "It is not a shield like one that you stick out in front of you. It is like a plexiglass shield that goes all the way around you. It is created by the force of the Word of God that abides in you."

You can walk right out in the midst of the curses, and they will run off of you like water off of a duck's back. But if you ever get within a mile of a blessing, it will run you down and overtake you.

People will say, "Why, that person must be the luckiest guy in the world." I don't believe in luck. I believe in the anointing and the shield of faith.

## God's Word for You Today

**PSALM 5:12 NASB**

**For You bless the righteous person, Lord, you surround him with favor as with a shield.**

## Give Voice to God's Word

*"Thank you, Lord, that you go before me today and make the crooked places straight. You surround me with favor as a shield. No weapon formed against me will prosper."* (Isaiah 45:2; Isaiah 54:17)

Day

9

# The Difference Between Principles and Formulas

**MARK 11:23**

**For assuredly, I say to you, whoever says to this mountain, "Be removed and be cast into the sea," and does not doubt in his heart, but believes that those things he says will be done, he will have whatever he says.**

People have the idea that all you have to do in the process of faith is to say a faith confession. While saying it is involved in working the principle, there is more involved. Keep in mind there are *principles* and there are *formulas*.

Let me give you an illustration. When my brother and I were very young, we were standing outside one day watching the birds fly off the barn. He said, "You know, if we had wings, we could fly."

I said, "Yeah, that's right."

He said, "I am going to go make us a set of wings."

He went into the house, and after a while, he came back with a set of wings. They looked like a set of perfectly good wings to me. They were two shoebox lids with a string tied around them. He was going to get up on the barn, fly down to our cousin's house, and land on his barn.

I said, "I want to go first!"

He said, "No, it is my idea, and I am going first."

I helped him up on the barn to the edge of the overhang.

He climbed up there and jumped off and went "thud" when he hit the ground.

I said, "Buddy, why didn't you flop your wings?"

He said, "I didn't have time!"

I said, "Give them to me. I know I can do it."

He helped me climb up the barn and I went up higher to the peak of the roof.

I was wearing a new pair of overalls that were just about four inches too long. I had them rolled up, but by the time he got me on top of that barn, they had become unrolled.

That barn was one of those old buildings that had those square nails. The top of the nails had worked themselves up a little bit on the edge of the roof. When I jumped off to have my maiden flight, one of my britches legs got hung on one of those nails. An angel just hooked it on there, I guess. I had plenty of time to flop. I was hanging upside down, just a flopping.

Now, the moral of this story is that things are not always like they seem to be. We had the formula down pat. All the birds did was kind of hop and flop their wings. We did that and went "thud." We did not have the principle.

This is what happens to a lot of people. They think, *All you have to do is say it.* That is part of the right formula, but the principle involved is you must believe and doubt not in your heart, and you must ***believe what you say*** will come to pass. Then, you shall have whatsoever you say. It is important to understand that.

## God's Word for You Today

**2 Corinthians 4:13 NASB**

**But having the same spirit of faith, according to what is written: 'I believed, therefore I spoke,' we also believe, therefore we also speak.**

## Give Voice to God's Word

*"I believe God's Word, and I use my faith to speak what He said about me. I am redeemed from the curse of sickness, poverty, anxiety, lack, and debt. God has set me free from the dominion of darkness and brought me safely into the Kingdom of His Son."* (Galatians 3:13; Colossians 1:13)

Day

10

# Words Create Images

**GENESIS 11:6 KJV**

**And the Lord said, Behold, the people is one, and they have all one language; and this they begin to do: and now nothing will be restrained from them, which they have imagined to do.**

You can only obtain what you can imagine. You conceive, or create an image, in your spirit by speaking, quoting, and proclaiming what God said in His Word.

Words create images. You can be sitting there thinking about something, and I can say, "freight train," and it will change the image in your mind. I can say, "airplane," and it will change your image again. Different spoken words create different images in your mind.

I remember when the Lord dealt with me along this line. I was walking up and down the airstrip out there where I had my airplane tied down. I walked down by the side of the airplane and then walked back up the airstrip about fifty yards. Then, I heard the Spirit of God say to me, "Now, why did you walk around that side of the airplane?"

I had no idea. You know, when the Lord asks you a question, it is not because *He* didn't know. It is because *you* didn't know.

I just stopped and stood there for a second or two. I turned around, and when I looked at that airplane, I had a flashback. I knew instantly why I had walked around that side of the airplane. Before I actually did it, *I saw myself* walking around that side of the airplane. That is the only reason I walked around that side of the airplane. That is the way we make decisions in life by doing what we see ourselves doing.

The Lord began to deal with me about the fact that if we keep God's Word in our mouths, speaking the things God said about us, we will *see* ourselves doing the right thing in life.

Have you ever said in a certain situation or circumstance, "I can never see myself doing that?" Your words create and reinforce the image of failure and impossibility in your mind.

But if you will speak the language of faith and agree with what God says about you, it will create an image of success!

## God's Word for You Today

**MARK 9:23 LSV**

**And Jesus said to him, 'If you are able to believe! All things are possible to one that is believing.'**

## Give Voice to God's Word

*"I do not let the Word of God depart from me, but I meditate on it day and night and act upon it daily. Therefore, I prosper and suceed in all that I do!"* (Joshua 1:8)

Day

# 11

# The Effects of Negative Words

**PROVERBS 4:24 RSV**

**Put away from you crooked speech, and put devious talk far from you.**

It's important not to speak contrary to what God says about you. If you have been poor-mouthing (talking about everything that is wrong), then a bad investment comes down the pike, you will probably feel led to go get involved in it.

Sometimes, you hear someone say, "You watch and see. I always get in on the bad deals. I never get in on any of the good deals." Their words create an image.

Then, these images develop into what they said. They see themselves losing out, and then they usually do.

Your words can have either a positive or negative effect on your life.

Whosoever shall say to the mountain (the situation or problem in your life), "be removed and cast into the sea" and shall not doubt in his heart and believe what he says shall come to pass, he shall have it.

What is he going to have? What he prayed? No, *what he said.*

If your saying does not line up with your praying, you are going to have what you say and not what you pray.

Your saying can undo your praying. I used to do that. I have been there and done that. I would go down to the altar, and pray, "Lord, just give me wisdom to make this decision. I just don't know what to do."

I would get up, and before I left the church house, somebody would say, "What are you going to do about that?"

I would say, "I don't have any idea. I am so worried." I got what I said, of course. Your words frame your world.

## God's Word for You Today

**JAMES 3:6 ESV**

**And the tongue is a fire, a world of unrighteousness. The tongue is set among our members, staining the whole body, setting on fire the entire course of life, and set on fire by hell.**

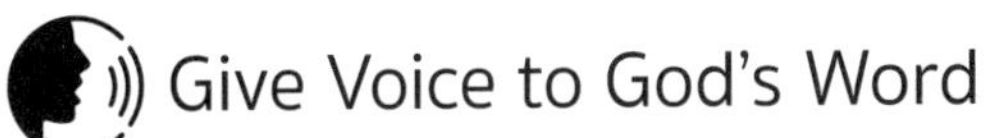

## Give Voice to God's Word

*"My words are the rudder to the ship of my life, and I cease speaking fear-filled, negative words. God's Word is in my mouth. It is alive, active, energizing, and effective in all the circumstances of my life."* (James 3:4; Hebrews 4:12 AMPC)

Day

# 12

# Stop Complaining and Say What God Said Over Your Situation

**JOHN 16:13**

**However, when He, the Spirit of truth, has come, He will guide you into all truth; for He will not speak on His own authority, but whatever He hears He will speak; and He will tell you things to come.**

When I got hold of this message of faith, I was like that poster that has a picture of a cat hanging on to the last knot at the end of a rope, that says, "Hang in there, Baby."

That is where I was. I was sick in body. I was head over heels in debt. I was supernaturally in debt. You could hardly get that way naturally.

Right after I heard that you can have what you say, if you believe and not doubt in your heart, I was praying one morning and telling the Lord what the devil said. I said, "Lord, things are not working out. Things are getting worse."

He asked, "Who told you that?"

It shocked me.

He said, "What are you doing, anyway?"

I said, "Well, Lord, I am praying." It almost insulted me that He did not know I was praying.

He said, "No, you are complaining. And I would appreciate it if you would quit coming to Me and telling Me what the devil said and calling it *praying*."

I said, "What should I do?"

He said, "Your problem is you pray too quickly."

That really took me back.

What He said was, "You would be better off taking a week, month, or year studying and confessing the Word until faith comes. Then, pray the prayer of faith, and you will get more prayers answered."

That is a good formula. I put that formula in motion after that. I can tell you that within the next three months, I got more prayers answered than I did the previous thirty years all put together. I started confessing the Word and kept confessing the Word until faith came.

Faith is in your heart and not in your head. Mental assent is in your head, but Paul said, "With the heart man believes." So, faith works in the heart, not in the head.

It changed my life when I started saying what God said. This message of faith and the principles of the Bible caused the biggest change in my life since I was born again and filled with the Holy Spirit. It was that major of a change.

## God's Word for You Today

**2 TIMOTHY 2:15 AMP**

**Study and do your best to present yourself to God approved, a workman [tested by trial] who has no reason to be ashamed, accurately handling and skillfully teaching the word of truth.**

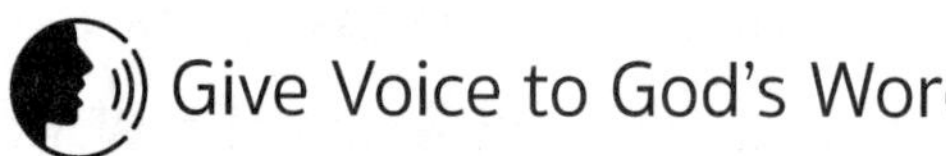

## Give Voice to God's Word

*"The Spirit of Truth dwells in me, and He teaches me all things and shows me things to come."* (John 14:17, 26; John 16:13)

Day

# 13 Stop Talking About Death and Dying

**PROVERBS 18:21 NIV**

**The tongue has the power of life and death, and those who love it will eat its fruit.**

When you begin to watch the things that you say, you start to listen to the way the world talks.

You start to hear things like:

"It tickled me to death."

"I laughed so hard I thought I would die."

"I'm gonna die if I go."

"I'm gonna die if I don't go."

"I am just dying to do so and so."

One guy said to me," I am just dying to go to Israel."

I said, "If I were you, I wouldn't go. Not with a confession like that."

You know, be reasonable about it. Let's say that you went to the doctor, and they gave you a prescription. Then, you went home and read on the label, "Take three of these a day until it kills you." What would you do with them? You would throw those things as far as you could throw them, wouldn't you?

Yet people will talk and say, "It tickled me to death," or "I laughed so hard I thought I was going to die." People are not going to die just because they said that one time, two times, or three times. But if they keep saying that, it will eventually catch up with them.

I heard one man at a Full Gospel Businessmen's meeting say, "I had better go home. Ha, ha, ha. The way my luck is running, I will probably get run over by a freight train by the time I get home."

I said, "I am not riding with you."

You see, he might get away with that and get lots of laughs. One day, it is a possibility that he will be led by his spirit to be on the train track when the 9:23 freight comes through one morning. He will get run over, and people will be saying, "We just don't understand why God took him. He was such a good Christian."

God would not have a thing to do with it. Man sets spiritual law in motion with his words. He receives what he continually speaks whether life and blessing or death and destruction.

## God's Word for You Today

**ROMANS 8:2**

**For the law of the Spirit of life in Christ Jesus has made me free from the law of sin and death.**

## Give Voice to God's Word

*"The law of the spirit of life in Christ Jesus has made me free from the law of sin and death. I speak LIFE to my body. With long life He satifies me, and I live the full span of my life in health!"* (Psalm 91:16; Exodus 23:26)

Day

# 14

# Applying the Principle of Faith to Your Life

## Separating From the Past

When you first read about Abraham in the Bible, his name was not Abraham. He was called *Abram*. Later, God changed his name to *Abraham*, which means "father of a multitude" or "father of many nations."

Abram's wife's name at this time was Sarai. God would later change her name to Sarah. *Sarah* means "mother of a multitude" or "mother of many nations."

**GENESIS 17:4–5 AMPC**

**4 As for Me, behold, My covenant (solemn pledge) is with you, and you shall be the father of many nations.**

**5 Nor shall your name any longer be Abram [high, exalted father]; but your name shall be Abraham [father of a multitude], for I have made you the father of many nations.**

**GENESIS 17:15–16 AMPC**

**15 And God said to Abraham, As for Sarai your wife, you shall not call her name Sarai, but Sarah [Princess] her name shall be.**

**16 And I will bless her and give you a son also by her. Yes, I will bless her, and she shall be a mother of nations; kings of people shall come from her.**

After God changed Abram's name to *Abraham*, he also changed Sarai's name to *Sarah*. He promised to bless her with a son who would be the promised child instead of Ishmael, the son of the handmaid. This promised child was to be named *Isaac*.

Abraham laughed when he heard God tell him this because he thought that he and Sarah were too old to have any more children. He was 100 years old, and Sarah was over 90. Again, God told him he was going to have a child from Sarah.

When Abraham was 100 he had known the promise of God for 25 years. Up until now there was no manifestation of the promise whatsoever. He questioned God saying, *"What will you give me seeing I go childless?"* (Genesis 15:2). He saw himself childless. He could not see himself with a child. God tried to get him to create the image by spoken words.

God had to instigate his law of faith. He changed Abram's name to *Abraham,* which means "father of a multitude." Every time Abraham and Sarah spoke their names to each other they would hear themselves calling each other the father and mother of a multitude. They would hear this over and over again. They would be calling out the promise of God every time they said each other's name.

## God's Word for You Today

**ROMANS 4:18, 21 WEYMOUTH**

**18 Under utterly hopeless circumstances he hopefully believed, so that he might become the forefather of many nations,...**

**21 ...being absolutely certain that whatever promise He is bound by He is able also to make good.**

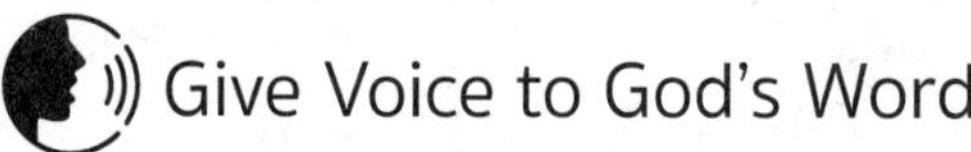

## Give Voice to God's Word

*"All the promises of God to me are yes and amen. God's Word is true. It cannot fail. It is working in me NOW!"* (2 Corinthians 1:20)

Day

15

# Doing Exactly What God Said to Do

## Why Is God Not Speaking to Me?

**GENESIS 12:1–2**

**1 Now the Lord had said to Abram: Get out of your country, from your family and from your father's house, to a land that I will show you.**

**2 I will make you a great nation; I will bless you and make your name great; and you shall be a blessing.**

God called Abram to leave his relatives and go to a new country. God promised to bless him, multiply him, and make his name great, and he would become a blessing to all the people of the earth. At this time, Abram is 75 years old.

When Abram first moved to the Promised Land he had taken Lot, his nephew, with him. God had told him to come out from among his relatives. Sometimes, you have to get away from your unbelieving relatives if you are going to believe God.

Abram did half of what God said. He did leave his hometown, but he ended up taking one of his relatives with him. He was trying to obey God like some of us do — following God but not perfectly. God deals with you where He finds you. Abram would eventually end up separating himself from Lot. Lot would choose to go in one direction, and Abram would go in another direction.

After Abram finally separated himself from his nephew Lot, God spoke to him again.

Sometimes the reasons we don't receive additional direction from the Lord is because we have not done *all* He told us in the first place.

**GENESIS 13:14–16**

**14 And the Lord said to Abram, after Lot had separated from him: Lift up your eyes now and look from the place where you are — northward, southward, eastward, and westward;**

**15 for all the land which you see I give to you and your descendants forever.**

**16 And I will make your descendants as the dust of the earth; so that if a man can number the dust of the earth, then your descendants also could be numbered.**

God promised Abram a physical land, the Promised Land, an area in the Middle East known as the Land of Canaan.

Today, our promises are the promises of a new covenant. The Bible promises found throughout the New Testament are our "Promised Land." I encourage you to find out what God has promised you and walk in it.

## God's Word for You Today

**GENESIS 13:17**

**Arise, walk in the land through its length and its width, for I give it to you.**

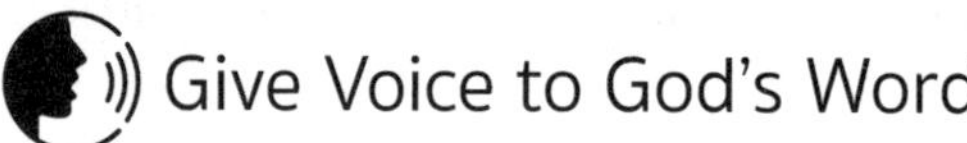

## Give Voice to God's Word

*"I am filled with the knowledge of God's will with all wisdom. I have spiritual understanding and follow God's direction for my life."* (Colossians 1:9 AMPC; 2 Peter 3:18 AMPC)

Day

16

# The Dynamo of the Law of Faith

In Romans chapter ten, the Apostle Paul tells you the way to get the Word of God into your heart.

**ROMANS 10:8 NASB**

**But what does it say? "The word is near you, in your mouth and in your heart" — that is, the word of faith which we are preaching,**

The Word of faith is first in your mouth and then in your heart. The more you say it, the more you believe it. The more you believe it, the more you say it. The more you say it, the more you believe it. It is like a dynamo — it just keeps generating power!

We call this the law of faith. Jesus tells us how to operate in this law.

**MARK 11:22–23**

**22 So Jesus answered and said to them, Have faith in God.**

**23 For assuredly, I say to you, whoever says to this mountain, "Be removed and be cast into the sea," and does not doubt in his heart, but believes that those things he says will be done, he will have whatever he says.**

Notice that Jesus said to say to the mountain to "be removed." Jesus did not tell us to speak to the mountain and say, "I will never get over you." Everybody talks about the mountain, but only a few people talk *to it* and *tell it what to do.*

Don't talk about your problems. Talk to your problems and tell them where to go. The devil will not stay around long if you keep the Word of God in your mouth. God's Word is the stabilizing force of your life.

## God's Word for You Today

**LUKE 10:19 ESV**

**Behold, I have given you authority to tread on serpents and scorpions, and over all the power of the enemy, and nothing shall hurt you.**

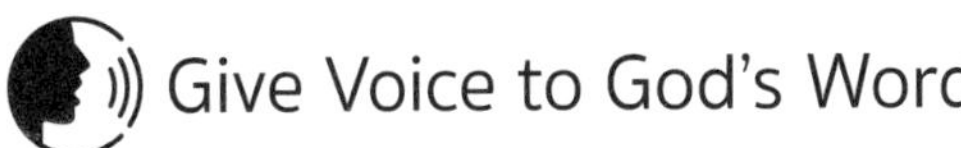

## Give Voice to God's Word

*"Jesus gave me authority over all the power of the enemy. I overcome evil with good and speak, 'Peace! Be still, in Jesus' name!'"* (Romans 12:21 ESV; Mark 4:39)

Day

17

# Give Voice to God's Word

**GENESIS 15:5–6 KJV**

**5 And he brought him forth abroad, and said, Look now toward heaven, and tell the stars, if thou be able to number them: and he said unto him, So shall thy seed be.**

**6 And he believed in the Lord, and he counted it to him for righteousness.**

God took Abram out and showed him the stars. He said, "Tell the stars, if you are able to number them ... so shall thy seed be." Well, you can see three or four thousand stars on a clear night![1]

[1]Miller, James, "How Many Naked Eye Stars Can Be Seen in the Night Sky?," AstronomyTrek.com, May 9, 2024, https://astronomytrek.com/how-many-naked-eye-stars-can-be-seen-in-the-night-sky/.

*"So shall my seed be."* That is what God had in mind. Speak to the stars. Tell the stars, "So shall my seed be." Abram was told to use an audible voice repeating what God had said to him about the stars.

When you confess the promise of God audibly with your mouth, it does something for the human spirit that nothing else does. I don't care how many other people say it. Their words will never affect you the way it affects you when you say it audibly with your mouth.

We have a little confession book that came out in 1976 called, *God's Creative Power® Will Work for You.* Over the years, it has sold millions of copies. But it is a *confession* book.

Sometimes, people will say, "Oh yeah, I read that book."

It is not a *reading* book. It is a *confession* book. It is a confession book because you say it. You say it audibly.

You need to give voice to God's Word. When you give voice to God's Word, that may be the only audible voice of God that you will ever hear. When you hear

God's Word spoken, it has a way of penetrating the human spirit and the human flesh. It will change your flesh. It will change you from the inside out.

The Lord said to Abram, "Tell the stars if you're able to number them." The Scripture says in the next verse, *"And he believed in the Lord and he counted it to him for righteousness."*

Did you know there are a lot of people who *believe in the Lord,* but they don't *believe what He said* about them? No, they don't believe the promises are for them now. They say, "Oh yeah, we're going to get that when we get to heaven." Will you need money to buy gasoline when you get to heaven? No, you need money to buy it now.

You see, it says Abram believed in the Lord and it was accounted to him for righteousness. God had to deal with him on his level. He will deal with you on your level as you advance in faith.

## God's Word for You Today

**PSALM 103:20 NASB**

**Bless the Lord, you His angels, mighty in strength, who perform His word, obeying the voice of His word!**

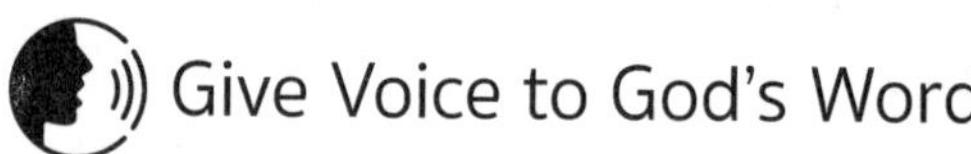

## Give Voice to God's Word

*"I am like a tree planted by rivers of water. I bring forth fruit in my season, my leaves do not wither and WHATEVER I DO PROSPERS. Angels go before me and prepare the way."* (Psalm 1:1–3)

Day

18

# Produced by Faith, Not Works of the Flesh

The next time the Lord appeared to Abram was after Abram and Sarai got together and decided that they were going to have to help God out.

**GENESIS 16:1–4**

**1 Now Sarai, Abram's wife, had borne him no children. And she had an Egyptian maidservant whose name was Hagar.**

**2 So Sarai said to Abram, "See now, the Lord has restrained me from bearing children. Please, go in to my maid; perhaps I shall obtain children by her." And Abram heeded the voice of Sarai.**

**3 Then Sarai, Abram's wife, took Hagar her maid, the Egyptian, and gave her to her husband Abram to be his wife, after Abram had dwelt ten years in the land of Canaan.**

**4 So he went in to Hagar, and she conceived....**

Have you ever thought God did not understand your situation?

They thought it was through Sarai's maid that they were going to have the promised child. Abram had a baby through Hagar and they named him Ishmael. Ishmael was not going to be the blessed child God promised them.

Ishmael was not a child they produced by faith. Ishmael was a result of what happened when they got over in the flesh and tried do things without God's help.

Abraham prayed:

**GENESIS 17:18–19**

**18 And Abraham said to God, "Oh, that Ishmael might live before You!"**

**19 Then God said: "No, Sarah your wife shall bear you a son, and you shall call his name Isaac; I will establish My covenant with him for an everlasting covenant, and with his descendants after him.**

He wanted Sarah's plan to work but God had another plan. When we try to *help* God instead of waiting for Him to perform His Word, we cause trouble for ourselves and others. Paul shows us that Abraham came to a place where he no longer wavered, "being fully convinced that what God had promised He was also able to perform." What God has promised *you*, He is perfectly capable and willing to perform.

## God's Word for You Today

**PHILIPPIANS 1:6 ESV**

**And I am sure of this, that he who began a good work in you will bring it to completion at the day of Jesus Christ.**

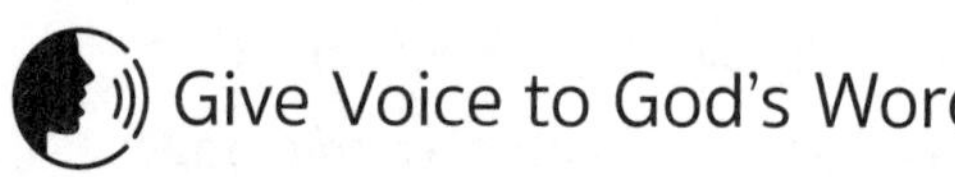

## Give Voice to God's Word

*"I declare that I will follow the leading of the Holy Spirit, and God's plan and purpose for my life will be fulfilled."* (Jeremiah 29:11; Isaiah 46:10)

Day

19

# Hearing and Renewing Your Mind

**ROMANS 10:17**

**So then faith comes by hearing, and hearing by the word of God.**

Faith comes by hearing and hearing and hearing. Hearing is in the continual tense. Someone would not walk up to somebody and say, "How is your heard." You might think they were talking about their cows, wouldn't you? You don't want to know how he heard last week. You want to know how he is hearing now.

Hearing is in the continual tense, and renewing of the mind is in the continual tense. The Apostle Paul said:

**ROMANS 12:2**

**And do not be conformed to this world, but be transformed by the renewing of your mind, ...**

You renew your mind with the Word of God by speaking the Word over and over and over audibly until the mind is renewed. It is a process that continues throughout your life.

You don't ever quit renewing your mind because you are rubbing up against people every day who will affect you negatively. You get around some folks for 25 minutes, and you'll be saying some of the ugly stuff they say. "Oh, we're just working ourselves to death." Then you'll catch yourself saying things like that. You have to renew your mind. Then, you have to *keep* your mind renewed.

## God's Word for You Today

**JOHN 15:3 KJV**

**Now ye are clean through the word which I have spoken unto you.**

## Give Voice to God's Word

*"I am clean through the washing of the water of the Word. My mind is renewed, and I am transformed into the image God created me to be."* (Ephesians 5:26; Ephesians 4:23)

Day

# 20 Calling Things That Are Not

## Get Supernatural Hope

God taught Abraham to call those things that were not until they were.

**ROMANS 4:17 KJV**

**(As it is written, I have made thee a father of many nations,) before him whom he believed, even God, who quickeneth the dead, and calleth those things which be not as though they were.**

What does it mean to call things that are not? Not what? They are not evident in the natural realm. They are things you cannot see, feel, taste, or touch.

Anything like a chair or a table is in the natural realm. You don't have to use faith to believe these things are real. You can touch them and feel them. I guess if you could bite them, you could taste them. They are in the natural realm. It does not matter whether you believe it or not. They are here.

You do not need faith for things you can already see. You use faith to bring the unseen into the realm of physical reality.

Romans chapter four goes on to talk about how Abraham believed in the hope of the unseen promise of God.

**ROMANS 4:18 KJV**

**Who against hope believed in hope, that he might become the father of many nations, according to that which was spoken, so shall thy seed be.**

Notice it says, *"Who against hope believed in hope."* In other words, when there was no hope in the natural, Abraham believed it. When you get to the point where you do not see any natural hope, you need to be like Abraham. Go to the Word of God and get ***supernatural hope.***

You should recognize your need to believe the Word. Look at and listen to the promises of God like Abraham did and allow them to create hope inside of you. Then you call those things that are not as though they were. Call it as though it already exists. By faith, you call yourself saved and baptized in the Holy Spirit. By faith, you call yourself healed, and by faith, you call all your needs met. By calling those things God promised as though they were, you will please God with your faith.

## God's Word for You Today

**HEBREWS 11:1**

**Now faith is the substance of things hoped for, the evidence of things not seen.**

## Give Voice to God's Word

*"I stand on the promises of God's Word, and I call myself healed. I call myself healthy. Body, listen to me. I am speaking to you. You are healed by the stripes of Jesus! I call my needs met. I do not lack health. I do not lack finances. God supplies* ***all*** *my needs according to His riches in glory by Christ Jesus."* (1 Peter 2:24; Philippians 4:19)

Day

21

# The Blessing of Abraham Belongs to You

We have a heritage of faith we can trace all the way back to Abraham. The Bible says that all who are in Christ Jesus are related to Abraham by faith. Those who have faith, no matter what race they come from, are considered children of Abraham.

If you have faith in the promises of God like Abraham did, you are justified by faith before God, and you will be blessed by God like Abraham.

**GALATIANS 3:6–9 KJV**

**6 Even as Abraham believed God, and it was accounted to him for righteousness.**

**7 Know ye therefore that they which are of faith, the same are the children of Abraham.**

**8 And the scripture, foreseeing that God would justify the heathen through faith, preached before the gospel unto Abraham, saying, In thee shall all nations be blessed.**

**9 So then they which be of faith are blessed with faithful Abraham.**

Abraham believed God and it was accounted to him for righteousness. By faith Abraham and Sarah had a promised child and they named him Isaac. Isaac had a son named Jacob. Jacob had twelve sons who became the twelve tribes of the nation of Israel.

The nation of Israel received the Law of Moses and the Ten Commandments directly from God. Along with the Law of Moses came blessings and curses. God said if the nation of Israel would follow and obey His laws, He would bless them. God warned them if they did not obey His laws they would be cursed.

**GALATIANS 3:13–14**

**13 Christ has redeemed us from the curse of the law, having become a curse for us (for it is written, "Cursed is everyone who hangs on a tree"),**

**14 that the blessing of Abraham might come upon the Gentiles in Christ Jesus, that we might receive the promise of the Spirit through faith.**

The term "curse of the law" refers to the consequences that came to those who did not obey God's laws. When you broke one of God's laws, the only way to avoid the curse of the law in the Old Testament was to come before God to receive forgiveness. Forgiveness came by an elaborate system of sacrifices made by the appointed priests according to the laws and ordinances set down by Moses.

The Old Testament is full of types and shadows of things to come. These sacrifices and rituals served a purpose, but they were not a permanent solution to pay for the sin of the world. They had to be repeated over and over again.

The types and shadows of things to come would find fulfillment when God sent His Son, Jesus Christ, to be the final sacrifice for the sin of the world. When John the Baptist saw Jesus Christ, he recognized Him as the promised Messiah, the one who would take away the sin of the world.

## God's Word for You Today

**ROMANS 6:7 NLT**

**For when we died with Christ we were set free from the power of sin.**

## Give Voice to God's Word

*"I am free from the power of sin, sickness, and disease. Sin and sickness have no dominion over me. The resurrection power of Christ dwells in me, and I am alive unto God."* (Romans 6:11, 14 ESV)

Day

22

# Taking Away Sin and the Curse

**JOHN 1:29**

**The next day John saw Jesus coming toward him, and said, "Behold! The Lamb of God who takes away the sin of the world!"**

Jesus Christ's death on the cross in Jerusalem 2,000 years ago would satisfy God's judgment against sin once and for all. His death on the cross would make it possible for all men and women everywhere to be reconciled to God by faith and to have all their sins forgiven. There would not be any need for further sacrifices for them to be made right with God.

This final sacrifice of Jesus Christ would justify anyone who received by faith what He accomplished for them when He died.

**2 CORINTHIANS 5:21**

**For He made Him who knew no sin to be sin for us, that we might become the righteousness of God in Him.**

When you have faith in Jesus Christ, you become the righteousness of God. In other words, you now have rightstanding with God because of His death. God substituted and placed on Him the judgment you deserved.

Jesus Christ's death on the cross enabled you to have your sins forgiven. There is nothing standing in the way between you and the blessing of God. When you receive this righteousness by faith, you are redeemed from the curse of the law.

**GALATIANS 3:13–14**

**13 Christ has redeemed us from the curse of the law, having become a curse for us (for it is written, "Cursed is everyone who hangs on a tree"),**

**14 that the blessing of Abraham might come upon the Gentiles in Christ Jesus, that we might receive the promise of the Spirit through faith.**

Those who have faith in Jesus Christ are redeemed from the curse of the law and are entitled to the blessing of Abraham. This blessing can now be received by anyone who, like Abraham, has faith to receive it.

Faith in Jesus Christ and your position of righteousness in Him has made all the promises of God available to you by faith.

## God's Word for You Today

**DEUTERONOMY 28:8**

**The Lord will command the blessing on you in your storehouses and in all to which you set your hand,...**

## Give Voice to God's Word

*"I am blessed in the city and blessed in the field. I am blessed everywhere I go and in everything I do. The Lord causes all that I do to prosper."* (Deuteronomy 28:1–4)

Day

# 23

# The Righteousness of Faith Speaks

**ROMANS 10:6–7**

**6 But the righteousness of faith speaks in this way, "Do not say in your heart, 'Who will ascend into heaven?' " (that is, to bring Christ down from above)**

**7 or, " 'Who will descend into the abyss?' " (that is, to bring Christ up from the dead).**

You might say, "Who in the world would say that?" But we have all said it in one way or another. If you have ever said, "Lord, if You will just come down and touch me, I would get healed," then that is basically what you have said.

It would seem you want to reverse the process of death and get Jesus back into His flesh, bone, and blood body so that He could lay hands on you and minister to you the way He did before He was crucified. If Jesus came back again, then you think you could get healed.

What Paul is referring to here is that after Jesus rose from the dead and had His glorified body, He never healed another single person. He never cast out another demon. He never did a single miracle by the laying on of hands.

Why? He lost His right to operate as a man. While He was down on the earth, He was operating as a man who was anointed with the Holy Ghost. He was the Son of God, all right, but He had a physical flesh, blood, and bone body.

The Apostle Paul said, "The righteousness of faith wouldn't say if Jesus would come back, reverse the process of death, and return to being in a physical body where He had the authority to destroy the works of the devil, then everything would be okay."

He said, "The righteousness of faith would not say that."

What would it say?

**ROMANS 10:8**

**But what does it say? "The word is near you, in your mouth and in your heart" (that is, the word of faith which we preach):**

The righteousness of faith would speak the Word of God, the word of faith that is in your heart. You do not need Jesus to come back to the earth from heaven to do this. You have to speak the words of faith yourself.

**ROMANS 10:9–10**

**9 That if you confess with your mouth the Lord Jesus and believe in your heart that God has raised Him from the dead, you will be saved.**

**10 For with the heart one believes unto righteousness, and with the mouth confession is made unto salvation.**

The righteousness of faith speaks the word of faith that comes from your heart and brings about your salvation. The Greek word for "salvation" here is the verb *soteria*. In other places in the Bible, the Greek word for "salvation" is the noun *sozo*. Both these Greek words mean "deliverance, preservation, healing from temporal evils and all other things." It is an all-inclusive word.

You are born again by believing in your heart and declaring it with your mouth. If you want deliverance from evil, sickness, disease, and other things that come upon you in life, you had better get your mouth in motion — and get those promises spoken. Believe it and speak it!

## God's Word for You Today

**2 CORINTHIANS 4:13 NIV**

**It is written: "I believed; therefore I have spoken." Since we have that same spirit of faith, we also believe and therefore speak,**

## Give Voice to God's Word

*"I am an overcomer, and I overcome by the blood of the Lamb and the word of my testimony."* (Revelation 12:11)

Day

24

# Abraham Gained Access to God's Grace by Faith

Faith does not work alone to receive God's promises. Faith and grace go together. You gain access to God's grace by faith.

**ROMANS 4:16**

**Therefore it is of faith that it might be according to grace, so that the promise might be sure to all the seed, not only to those who are of the law, but also to those who are of the faith of Abraham, who is the father of us all.**

*"Therefore it is of faith, that it might be according to grace."* That statement reveals that the only way you

can enter into grace is through faith. You cannot get there any other way.

You cannot get there by being good or by doing good things. Although, you ought to do good things if you're born again. The only way you can get access to the grace of God is through faith.

**ROMANS 5:1–2**

**1 Therefore, having been justified by faith, we have peace with God through our Lord Jesus Christ,**

**2 through whom also we have access by faith into this grace in which we stand, and rejoice in hope of the glory of God.**

In these two verses and in other writings by the Apostle Paul, you see this over and over again: the only way you can access the grace of God is through faith.

You cannot do it on your own merits. It is important that you realize it is the grace of God that gets you through life. It is God's grace that makes His promises sure.

It is important to recognize that you cannot receive anything because you *earned* it. You receive blessing from God because He is full of grace. Your faith gives you access to God, but it is by grace that you receive what you need from Him.

## God's Word for You Today

**ROMANS 11:6 AMPC**

**But if it is by grace (His unmerited favor and graciousness), it is no longer conditioned on works or anything men have done. Otherwise, grace would no longer be grace [it would be meaningless].**

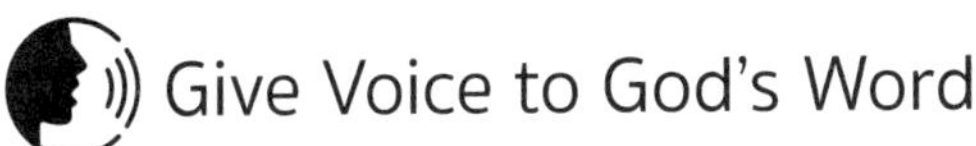

## Give Voice to God's Word

*"I am the righteousness of God in Christ Jesus, and grace reigns in my life."* (2 Corinthians 5:21; Romans 5:21)

Day

25

# Saying What You Already Have Is Not Faith

**MARK 11:23 KJV**

**...That whosoever shall say unto this mountain, Be thou removed, and be thou cast into the sea; and shall not doubt in his heart, but shall believe that those things which he saith shall come to pass; he shall have whatsoever he saith.**

There's always somebody who says, "Well now, Brother Capps, I just believe it this way. If you say it any other way than it is, you are just lying. You are just lying if you say you are healed when you are sick."

Think about this. The Bible says you can have what you say if you believe and doubt not in your heart. Some people go around saying things like, "I am sick." "I am sick as a horse." "I believe I am coming down with the flu." You hear people saying all kinds of things like that.

I was in a barber shop in England, Arkansas, getting my hair styled, and this old guy came in there coughing and sneezing. He said, "I have been trying to take the flu for three weeks."

I sat there and thought, *You know, if he has been trying to take it that long, he ought to have it.* He should have been trying to take a healing. People say those things and think it is just a funny thing to say. No, it causes reality.

Jesus Christ was not just making up Scripture to fill in the Bible when He said, "He will have whatever he says."

Jesus Christ did not say this to make it true. He said this because it was already true. He was just letting us in on it.

When you are speaking words, you are sowing seeds. You sow the seed and it makes demands of the soil. The soil has no choice but to respond to it. In the parable of the sower, the ground was referring to the heart of man, not the blood pump, but the core, the center of your being. We can substitute "spirit" for "heart." Your spirit, or heart, will bring about, or lead you to receive, what you have confessed

One of the missing links in the faith connection is that people do not spend the time to tame their tongue and get their vocabulary straightened out. It takes weeks and sometimes months to do that. I am not telling you that it is an easy thing to do.

If you are going to operate in the principles of the law of faith, it is a must. You must spend the time to get the Word of God in your heart in abundance. That is what Jesus is talking about. That is where the power is.

## God's Word for You Today

**PROVERBS 8:6** AMPC

**Hear, for I will speak excellent and princely things; and the opening of my lips shall be for right things.**

## Give Voice to God's Word

*"I submit myself to God, and the devil flees from me because I resist him in Jesus' name."* (James 4:7)

Day

26

# God Created the Visible From the Invisible

Everything that is made reveals the principles of God. The Apostle Paul said in Romans chapter one:

**ROMANS 1:20 KJV**

**For the invisible things of him from the creation of the world are clearly seen, being understood by the things that are made,...**

You can take a copy machine and put an open Bible on it, punch a button, and out comes a copy. You do not have to proofread the copy. Why don't you have to proofread the copy? Because it is an exact duplicate of the original. Every "i" is dotted. Every "t" is crossed.

If somebody types that page, you better proofread the copy because mistakes can be made.

How do you know the copy machine will make a duplicate of the original? Copy machines make duplicates of the originals 100 percent of the time. That is what they are designed to do. All the duplicates on a copy machine look exactly alike.

There is a law of faith. If you operate in the law of faith properly, it will work 100 percent of the time. The law of faith will produce the same results over and over again. We are not perfect in everything, but we strive for perfection. Personally, I have learned some things about the law of faith that will short it out and some things that will help it along.

Study the Word concerning the law of faith. Allow the Holy Spirit to reveal it to you and become skilled and proficient in your walk of faith. As you meditate the promises, they duplicate in your heart and become a part of you.

## God's Word for You Today

**2 CORINTHIANS 3:18 BLB**

**And we all having been unveiled in face, beholding as in a mirror the glory of the Lord, are being transformed into the same image, from glory to glory, even as from the Lord, the Spirit.**

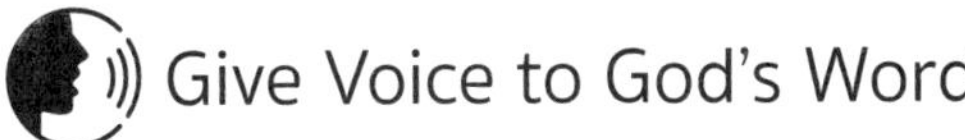

## Give Voice to God's Word

*"I have put off the old man and have put on the new man, which is renewed in the knowledge after the image of Him that created me. I am filled with the knowledge of the Lord's will in all wisdom and spiritual understanding."* (Colossians 3:10; Colossians 1:9)

# Day 27

# Words, Faith, and Things

**MATTHEW 12:34**

**...For out of the abundance of the heart the mouth speaks.**

I have a teaching series called *Words, Faith, and Things*. God's Word produces the faith for the things that God has already provided for you. You must *confess the Word* until faith is abundant in your heart. Then, when faith is abundant in your heart, you *speak words* of *power* that change situations and circumstances.

There is an anointing there. The power of God surrounds you. You can walk out into the midst of the curses, and they will run off you like water off a duck's back. If you get close to a blessing, it will overtake you. It is coming so much faster than you are going it will come upon you.

But you see, it takes time to develop that. That is one of the missing links in the faith connection. I see that people do not take their words seriously. Until you do that, it just kind of falls apart. It has to be in your heart in abundance.

Now, the guy that says, "Bless God, I believe you just have to say it like it is. If you say anything else, you are just lying." But just follow that guy and see if he believes that anywhere except in church. Now, see, that sounds good, naturally.

I bought a farm one time that was overgrown with Johnson grass. What if I had said, "Well, you know you have to plant it like it is. We are going to have to plant Johnson grass on that farm." Does that make any sense to you? No, that does not make any sense at all, does it? No, you plant cotton or soybeans or something. On the farm, we would never say, "We have to plant it like it is."

You don't have to say it like it is. You say it the way the Word says it is until you get what the Word says. It takes effort, but I can tell you it will work if you put in the effort to do it.

## God's Word for You Today

**DEUTERONOMY 28:2 ESV**

**And all these blessings shall come upon you and overtake you, if you obey the voice of the Lord your God.**

## Give Voice to God's Word

*"The Lord causes my enemies who rise up against me to be defeated before my face."* (Deuteronomy 28:7)

Day

28

# What Are You Calling?

**ROMANS 4:17 MSB**

**...the God who gives life to the dead and calls into being what does not yet exist.**

The guy who says, "Bless God, I just believe in *saying it like it is*, and if you say anything else, you are lying," will go home after church and walk out on his porch to feed the dog. He stands out there on that porch saying, "Here, Max! Here, Max!" However, Max is not in the yard. The dog is somewhere else.

I am going to ask him, "Why are you lying about your dog? Your dog is not here. Your dog is somewhere else."

The man said he believes in *calling it like it is*. Why didn't he go out there and call, "Somewhere, Max! Don't know where, Max." When the dog doesn't come, the man will end up thinking that it's not God's will for him to feed his dog.

For everything else in life, we ***call what we want.*** When lunch is ready but the kids are in the yard playing, you don't sit down at the table and say, "I guess it is not God's will that they eat lunch." No, you call them, and they will come. And you had better get out of the way because they will come quickly.

Now, let's say the guy goes out there to feed the dog, but the cat is on the porch. Because he has to call it like it is, he calls the cat. "Here, Kitty, Kitty." Then all the neighbor's cats come over.

The neighbor looks over the fence and says, "What are you doing with all those cats?"

The man says, "Well, I don't know. I am trying to feed the dog."

"If you are trying to feed the dog, why are you calling all those cats?" the neighbor asks.

He says, "Well, you have to *call it like it is*. When the cat is here, you have to call the cat."

Now, you laugh, but some of you have been doing the same thing.

Some people have said, "If we ever save any money, all the kids will come down sick, and we will have to spend every dime on doctors' bills. It happens this way every time."

That's like calling the cat when you really want the dog.

Do you see what I'm talking about? If you're not careful, you will fall right into *calling it like it is* instead of *calling for what you want*.

## God's Word for You Today

**MARK 11:24 LAMSA**

**Therefore I say to you, Anything you pray for and ask, believe that you will receive it, and it will be done for you.**

## Give Voice to God's Word

*"Christ has redeemed me from the curse of the law. For poverty, He has given me wealth. For sickness, He has given me health. For death, He has given me eternal life."* (Galatians 3:13; Deuteronomy 28)

Day

29

# Set Your Destination

**HEBREWS 11:1 KJV**

**Now faith is the substance of things hoped for, the evidence of things not seen.**

So, this guy who believes in calling it like it is, let's say he goes off on vacation and leaves his house shut up. He comes home, and it is 100°F in there. Well, he walks over to the thermostat and says, "Wow, it sure is hot in here. I believe in calling it like it is. I am going to set the thermostat on 100°F."

Then he calls the air conditioning man and says, "Get down here and fix this air conditioner."

The repairman says, "What is wrong with it?"

He says, "It is 100°F in here."

The repairman says, "Well, there is sure something wrong. We will get down there and take a look at it. Oh, by the way, what do you have your thermostat set on?"

He replies, "I have it set on 100°F. I believe in calling it like it is."

This same man thinks you are a nut if you call yourself healed when you're sick. But, he will walk over there to that thermostat and set it on 70°F when it is 100°F and feel real good about it. But if you say you are healed when you are sick, he thinks you are a little loony. Do you see the principle? That is why Jesus took natural things to show you spiritual things.

## Thermostats Are Goal-Setters

In an air conditioning and heating unit, the ***heart*** of the unit is outside the building. There is a thermostat on the wall. The thermostat is the goal-setter, as is ***hope***.

Paul taught that faith works in the ***heart*** and not in the head. I heard Brother Kenneth E. Hagin say, "You can have faith in your heart and doubt in your head, and it will still work." You cannot have faith in your head and doubt in your heart. That is mental assent.

The thermostat (***hope***) is simply a goal-setter. Whatever you set it on, that's what it will produce. It sends an impulse to the unit that says, "Get some cold air in here. We're hot."

Now, it will not cook your food or wash your clothes, but it will heat and cool your building. It is designed to do that. When you set 70°F on it, and it is 85°F in there, you have created a problem for the ***heart*** of that unit, but *it knows how to solve it.*

The thermostat is a set point for what you ***hope*** for, but the heart of the unit has the substance to heat or cool. Set your destination by calling for healing and release the substance of faith in God's promises.

## God's Word for You Today

**MATTHEW 8:17 AMP**

**So that He fulfilled what was spoken by the prophet Isaiah: "He Himself took our infirmities [upon Himself] and carried away our diseases."**

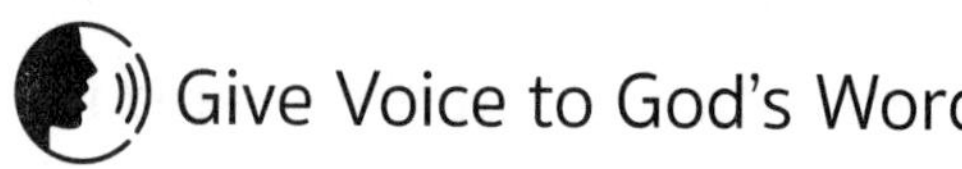

## Give Voice to God's Word

*"You have given me abundant life. I receive that life through Your Word, and it flows to every organ of my body bringing healing and health."* (John 10:10; John 6:63)

Day

30

# Your Mouth Is a Goal-Setter

**ROMANS 10:8–9**

**8 But what does it say? "The word is near you, in your mouth and in your heart" (that is, the word of faith which we preach):**

**9 that if you confess with your mouth the Lord Jesus and believe in your heart that God has raised Him from the dead, you will be saved.**

When you speak audibly, it sends an impulse into your heart. Your voice is picked up by the inner ear and fed right into the heart and plants the seed that says, "Find a way for abundance to come about."

The human spirit will search the avenues of God's wisdom — during the day, at night, and even while you are sleeping. It goes into search mode. Your spirit says, "Find a way to cause this to come to pass." You will be led by your spirit to be in the right place at the right time for the right situation. I have seen it happen time and time again. When you keep the right seed planted, your heart will find a way for it to come to pass.

The substance for heating and cooling a building is in the heating and air unit at all times, but it does nothing until you call for it. You can pray for weeks and months that the air conditioner will come on and that it will get cool in here. You can fast and pray, and nothing is going to happen until you act on what you know to do.

You can pray for all kinds of things. But if you are confessing what the devil says or saying, "The devil always does this and that and the other," you are giving him the preeminence. You'll never get the situation under control. The one thing that will bring it under control is God's Word spoken out of your mouth.

You can't go to the hardware store and buy one of those thermostats and nail it on your cabin wall in the middle of the woods where you don't have electricity and get it to work. I think that is what some folks have done when they say, "All you got to do is say it."

There is a lot more to it than saying it, but saying it is involved in working the principle. You speak the Word of God. You proclaim the Word of God.

It is like that airplane going down the runway. The faster it goes, more lift is created on the wings. God's Word spoken out of your mouth creates faith in your heart. It is *"in your mouth, and in your heart (that is, the word of the faith, which we preach"* (Romans 10:8).

Why won't the thermostat heat and cool a building by itself? There is no substance in that thermostat. There are two things in a thermostat box. There is a thermometer there for one purpose and one purpose only, and that is to tell you how hot it is right now. The thermometer will change with every wind that blows.

We have a lot of thermometer Christians. They can tell you how it is. It changes every time you hear them, except that it gets a little worse most of the time.

We need some thermostat Christians. They can change it. If you get the goal set with the words you speak from down in your heart, you are planting seeds in your heart, and your heart says, "Find a way for that to come to pass."

## God's Word for You Today

**ZECHARIAH 4:6–7 NLT**

**6 ...This is what the Lord says to Zerubbabel: It is not by force nor by strength, but by my Spirit, says the Lord of Heaven's Armies.**

**7 Nothing, not even a mighty mountain, will stand in Zerubbabel's way; it will become a level plain before him! And when Zerubbabel sets the final stone of the Temple in place, the people will shout: 'May God bless it! May God bless it!'**

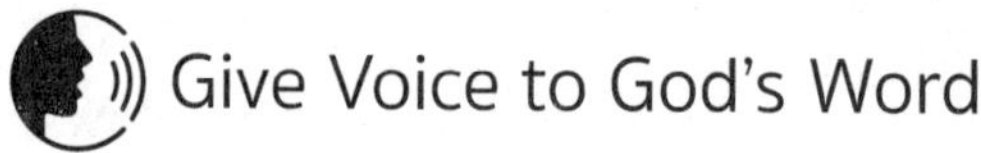

## Give Voice to God's Word

*"The Lord of Heaven's Armies is on my side! Not by might nor by power but by the Spirit of the Lord, this mountain comes down!"* (Mark 11:23–24)

Conclusion

# Your Heart Will Search for a Way to Meet Your Need

I know some of your thinking, "Now, where in the world do you get all this heart search stuff?" I am glad you asked. Look at Psalm 77:1–15:

> **1 I cried out to God with my voice — to God with my voice; and He gave ear to me.**
>
> **2 In the day of my trouble I sought the Lord; my hand was stretched out in the night without ceasing; my soul refused to be comforted.**
>
> **3 I remembered God, and was troubled...**

A lot of folks are troubled when they remember God. Pay attention to this:

**3 ...I complained, and my spirit was overwhelmed. Selah.**

Do you want to overwhelm your spirit? Complain.

**4 You hold my eyelids open; I am so troubled that I cannot speak.**

Then, you get to the point where you cannot confess the good things.

**5 I have considered the days of old, the years of ancient times.**

**6 I call to remembrance my song in the night: I meditate within my heart...**

This is what you are doing when you are confessing the Word of God. You are communing with your own heart.

**6 ...and my spirit made diligent search.**

There it is right there. "*My spirit made diligent search.*" Now, what was it that he communed with, and what did it bring?

**7 Will the Lord cast off forever? And will He be favorable no more?**

Now, this is what he made a diligent search about. It is telling you what the heart may diligently search about.

> **8 Has His mercy ceased forever? Has His promise failed forevermore?**
>
> **9 Has God forgotten to be gracious? Has He in anger shut up His tender mercies? Selah**
>
> **10 And I said, "This is my anguish; But I will remember the years of the right hand of the Most High."**

He got a revelation right there, didn't he? I caused this mess by the way I have been thinking and talking. This is my infirmity. But I will remember the years of the right hand of the Most High.

Now, he is going to think differently.

> **11 I will remember the works of the Lord; surely I will remember Your wonders of old.**
>
> **12 I will also meditate on all Your work, and talk of Your deeds.**
>
> **13 Your way, O God, is in the sanctuary; who is so great a God as our God?**

> **14 You are the God who does wonders; You have declared Your strength among the peoples.**
>
> **15 You have with Your arm redeemed Your people, the sons of Jacob and Joseph. Selah**

He talked himself right out of depression into blessing. His heart made a diligent search of God's faithfulness.

When you set that goal-setter, it sends an impulse and releases the substance in the heating and air conditioning unit. It will work day and night until it brings what you set in the goal-setter.

When you speak words that agree with God's Word, your spirit will make diligent search in the night to find a way to cause you to be in the right place at the right time for the right situation. Sometimes, it will steer you away from the bad deals.

You see how Jesus has used natural things to show you spiritual things. You plant a seed, and you reap a harvest. When you speak the Word, you are planting a seed. As you speak the promise of God, you are causing faith to come. The more you say it, the more you believe it. You call things that are not as though they were until they are.

Pray this with me, *"Father God, put a watch on my mouth. Let the words of my mouth and the meditations of my heart be on the promises and the blessings that are already given to me. I proclaim that I am blessed of God. I have the promises of God, and I plant the seed of God. So, I reap the harvest of God in my life. I call for abundance in the face of lack. I call for health in the face of sickness. I call forth the things that the Word says that I have, and I have what you say. Amen."*

## I Rest My Case

One day, I was standing at the pulpit, teaching. I said to the pastor on the front row, "Come here."

When he left his seat and stood in front of me, I asked him, "Why did you come up here?"

He said, "You called me."

"Oh, you sat there for over an hour and did not come. Why didn't you come a while ago?"

"Because you did not call me a while ago. You just now called me."

"You mean to tell me you were willing to come any time I called you?"

"Yes."

"But you did not come until I called you?"

"That's right."

"I rest my case."

# PRAYER OF SALVATION

God loves you — no matter who you are, no matter what your past. God loves you so much that He gave His one and only begotten Son for you. The Bible tells us that *"...whoever believes in him shall not perish but have eternal life"* (John 3:16 NIV). Jesus laid down His life and rose again so that we could spend eternity with Him in heaven and experience His absolute best on earth. If you would like to receive Jesus into your life, pray the following prayer out loud and mean it from your heart.

*Heavenly Father, I come to You admitting that I am a sinner. Right now, I choose to turn away from sin, and I ask You to cleanse me of all unrighteousness. I believe that Your Son, Jesus, died on the cross to take away my sins. I also believe that He rose again from the dead so that I might be forgiven of my sins and made righteous through faith in Him. I call upon the name of Jesus Christ and confess Him to be the Savior and Lord of my life. Jesus, I choose to follow You and ask that You fill me with the power of the Holy Spirit. I declare that right now I am a child of God. I am free from sin and full of the righteousness of God. I am saved in Jesus' name. Amen.*

**Charles Capps,** a farmer from England, Arkansas, became an internationally known Bible teacher by sharing practical truths from the Word of God. His simplistic and down to earth style of applying spiritual principles to daily life has appealed to people from every Christian denomination.

The requests for speaking engagements became so great after the printing of *God's Creative Power® Will Work for You* that he retired from farming and became a full-time Bible teacher. His books are available in multiple languages throughout the world.

Besides publishing 24 books, including best-sellers *The Tongue A Creative Force* and the *God's Creative Power®* series, which has sold over 9 million copies, Capps Ministries has a national daily radio broadcast and weekly TV broadcast called *Concepts of Faith.*

Although Charles has gone home to be with the Lord, his daughter, Annette, continues to carry on the legacy of his ministry.

**Annette Capps** is the President and CEO of Capps Ministries, an ordained minister, businesswoman, and licensed airplane pilot. Her diverse experiences have shaped her unique and practical approach to ministry. Combining the supernatural with the natural, her balanced message of the practical and the prophetic stirs faith in the hearts of audiences.

A lifelong student of the Bible, Annette has ministered across the nation and authored several books, including *The Spirit of Prophecy* and her bestseller *Quantum Faith*®. In addition to continuing the radio ministry of her father, Charles Capps, Annette hosts the *Concepts of Faith* television program.

In 2025, Annette launched Capps Chapel Radio on the Oasis Radio Network. Every weekday, she shares prophetic insight, practical truths, and powerful teaching designed to strengthen and encourage listeners in their walk of faith.

Coming from a long family history of farming, Annette maintains a close connection with the land by managing her family's farmland in Arkansas and Oklahoma. She and her husband live in Broken Arrow, Oklahoma, where the ministry is now located.

For a complete list of CDs, DVDs, and
books by Capps Ministries, write:

**Capps Ministries**
**P.O. Box 10, Broken Arrow, Oklahoma 74013**
*501-842-2576*

**cappsministries.com**

Visit us online for:

Radio Broadcasts in Your Area
*Concepts of Faith* Television Broadcast listings:
Local Stations, **Daystar, The Victory Channel**, & **TCT Network**

*youtube.com/CappsMinistries*
*facebook.com/CharlesCappsMinistries*

## BOOKS BY CHARLES CAPPS AND ANNETTE CAPPS

*Angels*
*God's Creative Power® for Finances**
*God's Creative Power® – Gift Edition**
(Now Available—Hardback Edition,
Vegan Leather Gift Edition, and Spanish Paperback)

## BOOKS BY ANNETTE CAPPS

*The Spirit of Prophecy*
*Overcoming Persecution*
*Reverse The Curse in Your Body and Emotions*
*Quantum Faith®**
*Removing the Roadblocks to Health and Healing*

*Also Available in Spanish

# BOOKS BY CHARLES CAPPS

*Calling Things That Are Not*

*Triumph Over the Enemy*

*When Jesus Prays Through You*

*The Tongue – A Creative Force*
(Now Available—Hardback Edition)

*Releasing the Ability of God Through Prayer*

*End Time Events*

*Authority in Three Worlds*

*Changing the Seen and Shaping The Unseen*

*Faith That Will Not Change*

*Faith and Confession*

*God's Creative Power® Will Work For You**

*God's Creative Power® For Healing**

*Success Motivation Through the Word*

*God's Image of You*

*Seedtime and Harvest**

*The Thermostat of Hope**

*How You Can Avoid Tragedy*

*Kicking Over Sacred Cows*

*The Substance of Things*

*The Light of Life in the Spirit of Man*

*Faith That Will Work for You*

*Also Available in Spanish

## Speak Life and Live Better, Stronger and Longer!

Join the millions whose lives have been changed by the *God's Creative Power*® Series. This dynamic series from Charles Capps has sold over 9 million copies. Each book reveals powerful teaching on the power of your words and includes scriptural confessions that will change the way you think and the way you live.

***God's Creative Power® Will Work for You***—*

Over 4 Million Sold!

Charles Capps' original mini-book reveals that the power of the spoken word can change your destiny. God created the universe by speaking it into existence. He has given the same ability to you through your words. To be effective in life, you must speak words of faith. Let faith-filled words put you over!

ISBN 13:978-0-9820320-6-0

***God's Creative Power® for Healing***—*

Over 4 Million Sold!

This powerful book combines all new teaching with Scripture confessions for healing. You will learn how you can release the ability of God for your healing with the words of your mouth.

ISBN 13:978-0-9820320-0-8

*Also available in Spanish